A Feather In The Breeze

Kushal Narang

ISBN 978-93-5667-154-6
© Kushal Narang 2022
Published in India 2022 by Pencil

A brand of
One Point Six Technologies Pvt. Ltd.
123, Building J2, Shram Seva Premises,
Wadala Truck Terminal, Wadala (E)
Mumbai 400037, Maharashtra, INDIA
E connect@thepencilapp.com
W www.thepencilapp.com

Author biography

Dr. Kushal Narang (b. 1980) is a cancer specialist by profession. He works at Medanta The Medicity hospital, Gurgaon. His passion for poetry dates to his school years, when the sights and sounds around his paternal home in Banaras Hindu University, Varanasi, inspired him to try this art.

He has previously published a collection of poems, The Innocent Years, in 2016. The present book, A Feather in the Breeze, includes poems written between 2016 and 2022.

CONTENTS

Epigraph

Wilder the storm, stronger shall be my tether !
But for the gentle breeze, I'll be a feather

Preface

This is a collection of poems written during the period March 2016 to February 2022, between the ages of thirty-five to forty-one of my life. I have classified them into five categories, namely Society and its Ways, Life and Death, An Alternate Take, Surrounded by Love, and Rhymes for Children.

The five poems on Society are as much based on interpersonal conflicts as they are on the response of society to certain specific situations, the dominant among these being the COVID-19 pandemic. Being a healthcare professional myself, it pains me deeply to see the disdain for rules and responsibility in the society, and our fraternity being ill-treated by public in general. A renaissance of social values seems to be the need of the hour.

The poems on Life and Death stem from adverse experiences and personal losses. Somehow, the belief grows strong in me that the world as we see through our eyes cannot be all that there is. Nature's processes often occur without explaining themselves, or rather, we are too small to experience or understand them completely. It feels soothing to imagine that there would be lives beyond the one we currently experience, some gifts waiting to be unwrapped even after we are done opening all of them, and some secrets yet to be revealed after we seemingly complete our journeys. Through my poems, I pay a small tribute to the beauty of life, and death - its counterpart.

An Alternate Take includes my own versions of popular fables, with my imagination running wild. A Twist in the "Tail" is the hare and tortoise story in a parallel world, while Eve's Apple narrates imaginary conversations about Biblical events and their contemporary relevance. The poem on Anatomy is intended to be a funny take on the perils of the subject as experienced by fresh entrants to medical schooling. The fact that I could recite it during our college reunion makes this one special for me.

The section Surrounded by Love is dedicated to my wife and daughters, and the beautiful world they have created for me. It is a blessing indeed to experience the warmth of love and companionship that they provide. Family-time with them is the most awaited part of my day indeed. Demanding attention and commanding respect on some occasions, while showering me with affection at other times, they really make me feel like "an island of blue, in a sea that's coloured pink !".

An extension of my fun-time with kids, as much as my academic responsibility towards them, is what constitutes the Rhymes for Children. Written mostly for my daughters' school performances, my rhymes touched me in the sweetest of ways when I heard them being recited in my children's voices. Truly, having your life-partner makes you feel close, but having children makes you inseparable !
Kushal Narang

Acknowledgements

A new phase of life, a new set of poems, and some more people to acknowledge. As I present my second book, life has moved on, some new people have entered, and some have left. And so, I have changed too, from being rather innocent to becoming a bit impure, from being a lot happier to becoming a bit morose, and from being blissfully ignorant to becoming a bit aware. Yet, I feel very much connected to and in love with the beautiful creation called Life.

Poetry continues to be my way of expression and has found a new meaning for me. With my dear wife Kavita sharing my zeal for the written word, and often providing me food for thought about lesser explored aspects, I find myself rejuvenated regarding my poetic efforts. My children, Anika and Avika, have added beautiful dimensions in my life and have helped me visualize aspects of my own childhood which I most certainly had either not registered in my memory, or completely forgotten about. Through their antics, and intelligence, they prove beyond doubt that we, as humans, continue to evolve and the newer generations are certainly improved versions of the past. Moreover, thanks to their academic requirements, I have been able to compose on topics that children may relate to more closely.

A poet cannot thrive without the encouragement and positive feedback he receives from his friends, who motivate him and continue to make him feel special and loved. I am thankful to all my friends for appreciating and understanding my poetry and propelling me towards pursuing my passion.

Time flows on, society continues to change, and that itself is inspirational in its own way. My colleagues at work, my patients, people, and their diverse thoughts in general, have had an impact on how I see myself, and the same is evident in my writings too. Besides, the entire world has seen some bizarre kinds of crises in the recent past. As we age, becoming a bit closer to God is natural. Hence, I find myself writing more about the process that life is, and what may exist beyond it.

May God bless us all.

Kushal Narang

Society, and its ways

<u>PARALLEL LIVES</u>

Private emotions, personal fears …
Existing in isolation over the years …
We hardly know how our brothers grew,
We hardly know what the others go through …

Healthy greetings return a grimace
Polite assertions become intrusion of space
All of others' virtues are taken as vices,
Efforts to unite cause identity crises…

We just keep running on parallel tracks
With eyes on our goal; ignorance behind our backs…
Crossing the hurdles in this steeplechase
Through life's complex, unrewarding maze.

Until Life itself interrupts this race
And decides to bring us face to face,

A Feather In The Breeze

Until our selfish predilections
Happen to cross at unpleasant intersections…

And oh, how strong is the interaction !
Extremely violent exothermic reaction !
Of ideas, beliefs, and pre-conceived notions
Exchanged with the other in unmeasured proportions !

The result is far worse than what did exist
Yet with our twisted beliefs we persist
What was earlier a wilderness of desolation
Looks more like a battlefield post devastation…

And so shall continue till the very end…
Our mutual hatred we shall never mend…
Only when the other's departed shall we ever realize
For the years he lived, he too paid the price…

Life's long gone now – what remains is the gist
That we could never really co-exist…
Alas, we had a chance to mingle so well,
Yet we preferred to be and stay *parallel*…

March 13, 2016

THE CREEPER

As many a wise man would opine
I am somebody without a spine
Frail, powerless, not worth a penny
My clingy creepiness a problem for many.

But what they miss, and fail to see
Is my eye for the supports surrounding me.
With the blueprint for progress crystal clear
I cling to my targets – so far, so near.

Not a mindless act it should seem to you –
I plan each move with strategies new
And what lies beneath each leap, every hop
Is my irresistible urge to reach the top.

With limited energy feeding my force
I strive to acquire each available resource…
With each new tendril that I do unwind
It sure takes away a part of my mind.

A Feather In The Breeze

But my efforts – the people – they so undermine,
My honest rapport they tend to malign
They won't work, won't stress, won't burn the sweat
And won't stop blabbering, just as yet !

Which is why I don't let their flip-flop
Dampen my march towards the treetop.
A creeper, as they say, shall I always be.
A climber, instead, is as I see me.

Shall bear each brunt with accustomed poise
Shall keep moving up without a noise
Wilder the storm, stronger shall be my tether !
But for the gentle breeze, I'll be a feather.

With my will to strive and keep striving on,
I shall survive while the others are gone.
All meaningless…. these silly fights…
As I do attain, unattainable heights !

November 11, 2016

<u>WHITE TIGER, MINUS THE STRIPES</u>

A timely "project" to its rescue
A salvage of national pride
When a dwindling tiger population
Was halted in its stride

So much for the jungle royal
Who heads the dietary chain
So much for the national symbol
Treated with disdain.

A similar royal, moves around
In supposedly civil surrounds
He bears a white coat, unlike it
And weighs much fewer pounds

Similar as his wilder mate
He heads the intellectual chain
Healing the ills and illnesses
With limited personal gain.

Why then is he whipped and beaten ?
Into a perilous state

A Feather In The Breeze

Why then is he so ill-treated ?
No project to rescue his fate ?

The law of the jungle expands, and so
Has reached our pearly gates
The so-called society is about to crumble
As Time patiently waits…

For if it so becomes the norm
To hurt the hands who heal and bless
Our end approaches with steadfast speed
And shall get us, nevertheless…

Make amends while there's time
Treat your healers the healthy way
They often die many times over
To make you live another day…

September 23, 2020

<u>DISCUSSIONS BEHIND THE MASK</u>

At a social gathering yesternight
With "socially distanced" folks
We sat for healthy discussions
And possible light-hearted jokes

Masked we were all when we began,
Following civilized norms.
But a few drinks having quenched our throats
We acquired uncivil forms !

I ventured about the benefits it brings
To be wearing a mask upright
Infection prevention, the obvious goal
But I had a deeper insight…

"Masking the face hides expressions
And often one's identity,
Masking the face conceals emotions
Or at least, emotional intensity."

A Feather In The Breeze

"Ha ! What's the big deal with that ?"
Barked a juiced-up case.
"Many are able to do just that
Without any mask in place !"

"They mask intent, personalities
Without a whiff around
They mask content and loyalties
Without the slightest sound !"

"But oh, this stifling mask indeed..."
Began a lady by the side.
"Blocks my breathing passages".
Adjusting her dress aside.

"Ask me", said a veiled maiden,
Accompanied by her spouse.
Clad from head to toe in black
And dying to share her grouse.

"Nothing new for those like us,
Who live behind bars unseen.
We're oft accustomed to suffocation
Of self and self-esteem."

A Feather In The Breeze

Quick to squirm was the spouse,
Hushing her up and away
While a glancing waiter moved aside
To get out of their way.

"Sir, please. Please check your mask.
Madam please take care..."
"Don't you let that barrier down,
You gentle folks beware !"

"It was just a week ago",
The waiter continued..
"I lost a dear one to a disease
That could not be subdued."

"It isn't just a mask to keep germs out,
It's a silent message instead.
That you do realize and support the efforts
That care-givers spearhead."

"I serve to earn my livelihood,
To keep my children fed.
But if I had the riches you got,
I'd stay at home instead."

"Pardon me, my blabbering tongue
Is unworthy of your time.
But I do really wish that all of you
Remain all fit and fine !"

Brought to senses all of us,
Stopped our discussions lame.
And prepared to head back to our dens,
With heads hung in shame…

January 8, 2021

<u>DARKEST TIMES</u>

Oft our older ones would say
Of dark and darker times bygone
I wonder how well these times qualify
As the darkest nights before dawn…

Thoughts of depression and doom prevail
Depleting our mental resource
The dance of disease and death dominates
Our residual working force

Calls and cries for help cumulate
Asking for care... and air
But alas ! We have nothing to provide
Just helplessness and despair

There are so many, fighting hard
There were so many who lost
There are some opportunist rogues as well
Busy multiplying the cost !

A Feather In The Breeze

Democracy sits pretty at the top
Watching the mayhem unfold
Unleashing draconian laws and more
Attempting to strengthen its hold

But one thing is clear, no doubt at all
That a society we aren't anymore
We care for self and self alone..
Socially-distant to the core !

Why then, it's a virus so small
That shows us our colours truest
With absent values and disdain for others
It sure is serving us the best...

The burden of humanity increases by the day
And yet we don't understand
That there is something grossly *wrong*
With the humans inhabiting this land

Oh, how shall all this mess be cleared...
How will our blunders be undone ?
We may think of possible ways,
But in reality there appears to be none !

We can only hope that the future is bright

Our next generations be blest !

And someday, we would tell young ones

That we lived through times darkest !

May 6, 2021

Life and Death

SEMI-CIRCLE OF LIFE

Do you just believe the daylight you see
And ignore the darkest night ?
Or do you just accept the warmth of summer
Keeping the winter out of sight ?

Can you hold time to stay in your favour
Or stop the receding tide ?
Or can you make the revolving planets,
Alter a single stride ?

Nature defines its processes perfect
In symmetrical, synchronous beats
What succeeds an event precedes another
Until the cycle repeats…

Why, and how, can life be any different
Or death, it's counterpart

A Feather In The Breeze

That stands at the far end of the journey
Just a lifetime apart…

There can't be no beginnings
There can't be no ends
Of a process that exists eternally
Of a curve that forever bends !

As night turns to day to night
As seasons merry-go-round
So do us through the circle of life…
And death, coming around

All our life-experiences
Stay vivid to the core
But what happens in after-life
Is a matter of faith, and more…

Men of science may fail to relate
Or accept the truth unseen
Of journeys trod on unknown paths
Of experiences serene…

But accept you do that energy exists
As dual particle-wave form

A Feather In The Breeze

And converting from one to the other
Is the acceptable norm !

So aren't we just particles in our life
And waves after we die ?
Until the time we re-particulate
As temporary passers-by…

We carry our traits across lives
A few memories as well
As we carry relationships
With whom we ever did dwell…

Perhaps that explains all deja-vu,
And the people who visit our dreams
Perhaps it explains how we connect
Across transcendental realms !

November 7, 2020

<u>KARMA</u>

Whatever happened…
To the truth, unspoken…
That promise, broken…
To the lies uttered
That mess, cluttered
To help, witheld
Those bonds un-gelled
You think they're unseen ?
All your deeds, unclean…

Whatever happened…
To the road not taken
That path, forsaken
To lesser beings, abhored
Those feelings, ignored…
To the words, unsaid…
Those letters, unread…
You think it was fair ?
Your not taking care…

A Feather In The Breeze

Whatever happened…
To lessons, unlearned
The care, unreturned
To that ever-mounting debt…
Of expectations, unmet…
To the harm, unintentional ?
Your views, self-preferential…
You think it's forgiven ?
Your life, misdriven…

It's all accounted, you fool !
Each mis-step, each vice !
And worth it will be…
Your karmic price !
January 10, 2021

<u>SOMEONE...</u>

A certain someone fathered me
A certain gave me birth,
A certain someone grew along
To make growing-up worth…
Numerous someones came across
A few of them stood-by,
Certain someones mentored me
And kept me aiming high…
A special someone married me
And loved me all my time,
Sweetest someones came from me
Brought happiness sublime !

Without these someones all around
Life's nothing but a sham,
And all of them have made me so,
The someone who I am…

January 23, 2021

<u>BUBBLES</u>

Ever seen bubbles...
Floating through the air
Carelessly, unplanned...
Going… rather being carried around
Through the whiffs of wind
And settling too,
Sometimes…

Rarely two, or more, combine
Coalesce into one…
Like conjoined twins
Or rarely still, the wall
That separates them
Dissolves…
Unifying their existence…

And then they continue
On their journey
Short-lived…
Until it's time for them
To burst…
And merge with the space
That gave them birth...

Eerily familiar…
Isn't it ?
Is life…

That you and I lead
As we float around
In endless space
Until our bubbles burst…

Nothing changes…
For what's around…
No void left behind
In the space
Endless…
By the bubble that's no more
Never was…

But that's not all…
Never will be
Reassemble it shall…
In a form afresh
Maybe with a bit more
Sturdiness…
Than the last time...

May 13, 2021

<u>DIVINE LIGHT</u>

My half-open eyes closed one night,
To enter that mystic realm
My psychic self was led miles away
By unknown forces at the helm

And soon my inward eye found me
Walking a familiar road
Strewn around with *Delonix*flowers
That once defined my abode

The eternally beautiful trees above
The air, so gratifying
The hope of making it big someday
The spirit gravity-defying !

When all at once a saw some light !
Approaching, as I stood
It brightened up, and soon assumed
The form of my old friend good...

A Feather In The Breeze

A part of me just held my ground
A part jumped with joy
A part of me raced right ahead
To hug that lovely boy !

For my brain reminded my saner self
That he was with us no more
But the heart sped ahead unrestrained -
Forever the sophomore !

"You bl***y this, you bl***y that ! ...
Where the hell you'd gone ?"
"Why didn't you tell me before, you brat
That you'd be gone so long !"

Of course that was how it had always been
Our manners of treating a guest
A barrage of abuses hurled across
To welcome our friends dearest

And he too, replied in a similar fashion
By planting a kick on my butt
"I don't need your permission, do I ?
You prickly, little nut !"

A Feather In The Breeze

But we soon embraced, and oh so hard
After our fake lambast
And we stood like that, embraced and all
Until some moments were past...

Tears of joy, of emotions heartfelt
Welled-up in eyes both ways
As we walked along as long-lost friends
Recounting bygone days…

We trod along the flowery path
That appeared lovelier, of late
And settled on the familiar stone plinth
That marked our hostel gate

"So, how have you been ?" I asked
"... and where exactly, as well...
In divine company, I'm sure." I said
But he said he could not tell...

"It isn't such a thing you all make it to be…
It isn't that much a deal !
"People like us are forever around...
Only if you care to feel..."

A Feather In The Breeze

"Of course, a physical presence is missed
By the laymen of your creed.
But perceiving our presence comes naturally
For those who care indeed."

"And it was you who said, isn't it ?
Of that human particle-wave form…
It isn't much different than that, you see…
You're watching me perform !"

"The light at the end of the tunnel, they say
Provides a glimmer of hope…
But to me it appeared similar to the one
At the end of the endoscope !"

"To each his own", he said
"The manner, the method, the time…
But crossing over from here to there
Is just a process sublime."

I listened to him with awestruck eyes
Watched mysteries unfold
As my divine friend from another world
Touched on issues untold…

A Feather In The Breeze

"You've moved way, way ahead", I said
Patting him on his back
"You've always had that extra spark…
That we mediocres lack."

"Cut the crap", he said with a smile.
"I have things at hand.
I don't have the whole day to spend
In this mortal-land !"

"But I'm not that far away too,
That I can't reach out to those
Whom I have kept close to my heart
And who like to keep me close !"

Saying this, he got up from there
And started gaining height
Then re-assumed his earlier form
Of that unflinching light...

Slowly the scene faded in my mind
And so did thoughts of gloom…
As I opened my eyes to a bright new day
With *Delonix* trees in bloom !

September 10, 2021

An alternate take...

<u>A TWIST IN THE "TAIL"</u>

...And so said the bird to the tortoise and hare
"Let me organize for you a deadly dare !
Where you shall race through water and fire
And I shall oversee as the Umpire"

"It will be a race that'll put you to the test
And your eternal rivalry shall be put to rest
Whoever shall triumph this one final bout
Shall be the undisputed victor, without a doubt !"

A ten-kilometer run was agreeable to all
Through a forest fire and a waterfall
Tempers flared... spirits were set ablaze !
As they prepared for the steeple-chase !

Judgement day came and the race began
With passion and fury, the runners ran...

A Feather In The Breeze

But so much were they into the race
That they missed the smirk on the bird's face…

As the fire roasted them black and blue
The triumphant bird over the trees flew
As the waterfall downsized their spirits to half
The bird barely resisted the urge to laugh.

A bitter lesson both the runners learnt
With scathed faces and fingers burnt
That maintaining a grudge serves a purpose no other
Than allowing a third to pitch one against another.

And so they both sat, reminiscing yesteryears...
Nursing each other's wounds through mutual tears
Very soon the writing was clear on the wall
That they were both nice persons after all !

They decided to forgive the bird's immoral act
For it's better to forget than overreact
The hare and tortoise persisted as friends very best
Their "eternal" rivalry was indeed put to rest !

March 17, 2016

<u>EVE'S APPLE</u>

"Shall we taste that far-flung fruit,
Forbidden for us by that brute ?"
"Brute He isn't, He's called God !"
Adam said with a vigorous nod.

"Of course he is !" replied Eve
As she stood and prepared to leave
"He made us of his own accord,
To be forever addressed as the Lord !"

"But I'm not the one so lame
To not be able to see through the game.
The fruit is the key to our ascent
Which no god ever, can ever prevent !"

And saying so, Eve took a mighty leap
To climb upon the tree-trunk steep
While Adam, confused, with a dropped jaw
Looked at her in shock and awe.

A Feather In The Breeze

"I got it ! I got it ! It's here !"
Eve rejoiced with a loud cheer
"This is **App**ealingly **ple**asurable", she said.
I guess I'll call it *Apple* instead.

Adam applauded on seeing Eve succeed
"That was a brave act indeed !"
But very soon he ceased to laugh
When Eve offered him the uneaten half...

"It's divine", she said. "I'm already wise".
"Won't my beloved share the prize ?"
Adam smiled, and ate the other part
And felt eternal bliss in his heart.

But the code of conduct had been breached !
And untold fury would now be unleashed !
Adam suddenly sensed a jinx
As the apple got stuck in his larynx !

The wave of fury was indeed surreal
As God's kingdom turned unreal
For the ones He had Himself created
For those who had so blatantly cheated !

A Feather In The Breeze

So, on moved Eve and Adam together
Through unforgiving time and unfair weather
And made a living of their own accord
With or without the blessings of the Lord.

But who was right and who was wrong ?
They pondered over this for long…
Was God right in denying them progress ?
Were they right in defying his process ?

Answers to these were never found
But time saw Earth with humanity abound
And so, we exist in the present day
With unknown blessings paving our way...

The apple, however retained its place
Snugly fit in that narrow space
Inside Adam's throat for ever
And for all of Adam-kind forever !

A reminder that life's no heaven indeed !
That joys and sorrows are of similar breed
It's important to swallow your guilt, and pride
And keep moving on from stride to stride…
August 11, 2019

<u>ANATOMY</u>

Walking smart with a confident stride
Riding high on the success tide
I suddenly felt a sting in my a**
As soon as I entered my Anatomy class !

The name indeed its nature fits
For the subject had my a** in splits
Just that the "a" that lies in middle embed
Is better replaced with "o" instead.

Posing with the skeleton was so cool !
While we were those nerds back in school
We wouldn't be scared - were it to roar,
But its individual bones could haunt much more !

Take the hip bone as an example
With holes, twists, and curves ample
What attaches on top or comes out from the bottom
Was something I found so hard to fathom

A Feather In The Breeze

Building your biceps is so easy-peasy
But its origin-insertion still makes me dizzy
Was it in December or was it in June ?
Did you use your gracilis, on your honeymoon ?

And do you remember those goddam nerves ?
Which sense it carries, which muscle it serves ?
Or the web of arteries supplying the brain ?
The veins, my blood, they flawlessly drain

The head and neck, most complex to recall
And the base of skull would top it all
Despite best efforts, I failed to relate
Which f***ing foramen did that nerve penetrate !

But most solid organs were a bit fine
Holding the heart was a feeling divine
Lungs and the liver, the silent giant
Self-regenerating, self-reliant !

The fossae, foraminae, the pouches and tubes
The surface contours, the axillae, the pubes
The vocal, the spinal, the spermatic cord
All so intricately designed by the Lord

Pardon my language, excuse my lies…

It's Anatomy only that made me realize

That we have so much inside our bod

This science indeed is the science of God !

July 31, 2020

Surrounded by Love

<u>AN EPIC LOVE-STORY</u>

It's been some lively yesteryears
Since I met my love-lyric
Two tiny angels blessed our lives
As our love-story turned epic !

But not so simple should it seem
To one who happens reading this
Fruitful rewards need stern efforts
And that is how this love-life is !

A lonesome, handsome somebody
I think I was, some point in time
A vibrant, fragrant flower was she…
Blooming in her youthful prime

Our feelings struck a rhythm divine
Thanks to our planets and stars

A Feather In The Breeze

But Venus was her preferred home
While I belonged to Mars !

A minor celestial rearrangement
Of tempers and temperaments galore
A little adjustment here and there
And we loved even more !

Love bore fruit in the loveliest way
An angel personified !
The apple of my eye indeed
My moment of fatherly pride !

And the fragrant flower that was her
Became Mother Nature herself
To bear and rear her treasured fruit
And raise her miniature self

While here was clumsy me instead
Balancing work and life
Servant to humanity, son to parents
And husband to my wife

Many a big, fat book I'd read
Oft managed a dreaded disease

A Feather In The Breeze

But oh, this new-found tiny-tot
Was beyond my expertise !

But look at her, just cruising along
Through work, and house and kid
And friends and kith-and-kins all
Much more than I ever did

Time flew fast and angel grew
Cuter and naughtier by the day
Through smiles or pranks or otherwise
She would have her way !

Until of course we found a route
To magnify our world
As another angelic presence formed
And destiny unfurled…

New joys galore she brought to us
And relief from a testing time
Her tiny, yet wholesome form perfect
Her ethereal beauty sublime !

So soft and sweet her charming self
So tranquil is her sound

A Feather In The Breeze

An experienced father is how I feel
With my second child around

And so, she grows too, so do us
In this journey of family-life
And grows along our story of love
Of daughters, man and wife !

I marvel at these big-small girls
Of different shapes and sizes
Who hold me in their loving fold
With sweet, naughty surprises !

I look again at my dear self
And can't hold back a grin
I thank the Lord for who I am
And the kind of life I'm in..

An agreeing husband, obedient father
With things in near-perfect sync
As I lay floating, an island of blue
In a sea that's coloured pink !
For my wife Kavita, on her birthday
June 4, 2020

THE FRUITFUL TREE

Out of fun and frolic one day
Involved with kids in childish play
I gave them a situation to analyze
A little, big mental exercise

"Imagine you have a fruitful tree,
Growing on your side of the fence.
But the fruits it bears tend to fall
Into the neighbour's occupance."

"The fruits are lovely, smell and taste
And you want to gulp them in all haste.
But the barbed fence you cannot cross
For stealing is a sin so gross !"

"The neighbour too has his moods
Depending on the time and day.
But smile he does, and broadly too
While picking the fruits in his way."

A Feather In The Breeze

"The tree needs your constant care
For without your help, it cannot fare
To be able to firmly establish its roots
To be able to blossom and bear fruits."

"So, what would you do in such a case
Where your efforts don't fetch an award
Where all your nurturing care and sweat
Doesn't return a fruitful reward ?"

The elder one bore a look of intent
Focused on the problem's content
While the younger one was more at ease
Fiddling with her ABCs...

"Why do you look only at the fruits ?"
Said the elder after a thought
"The tree would provide a pleasing shade
Whenever I'd be lonely and distraught."

"It's home sweet home for the birds who nest,
And a playing ground for all the rest."
"Our lonely neighbour, oft irked and rile
But picking the fruits does make him smile !"

A Feather In The Breeze

Still marveling at what the elder said,
I hinted a glance at my younger one
Who appeared to be busy in herself
Yet replied with an air of fun…

"Us, the neighbour, the fruits and the tree
Are all created by heavenly decree
Except the fence that holds us apart
And puts a leash around a loving heart."

"So I'll remove the barbed fence that stands
Betwixt us and our neighbour's lands
So that we exchange goodies galore !
Sharing fruits, and much much more !"

September 6, 2020

A DECADE OF TOGETHERNESS

A milestone of love & togetherness
Awaits us in the days to come
As you appear more beautiful !
And I seem a bit handsome :-)

It's a moment for us to celebrate
And cherish forever and more…
To design a lovely future
To relive the days of yore…

Ten years have passed by
Of growing up together as one
Ten years of singing
Sweet harmonies in unison !

And so, I want to gift you
A timeless flow of love
That keeps your heart brimming
As more comes pouring from above !

A Feather In The Breeze

Oh, how I wish to see you
Relishing your choicest treats
As I wish to see myself,
Attaining culinary feats !

I wish our sweetest children
Stay happy and naughty always
Making academic progress
While their childish charm stays :-)

My fair lady you will always be
The fact remains crystal clean
And the days to come will show you,
The beauty of what I mean…

February 14, 2021

Rhymes for Children

<u>MY DREAM INDIA</u>
(Through my daughter's eyes)

I'm a six-year-old girl today
But I'll grow to become a woman one day
And I wish my India grows-up too
To suit the needs of women today

I wish no girl child ever at all
Is deprived a life or livelihood
I wish she gets her education
As much as another boy would

I wish she feels fully secure
Of herself, mind, and body too
I wish she has the confidence
To do the things as she wants to

Of course, I want terrorism to end,

A Feather In The Breeze

Poverty to vanish, corruption to abate.

Of course, I want the environment

To return to its earlier, cleaner state

But more than all these physical changes

I wish India changes its mind

And treats its diverse cultures and people

As Indians, all being one of a kind !

An equality on all fronts is what I want
In the India of the dreams I see
And then shall all the men realize

What a six-year-old girl can be !

July 25, 2020

<u>SPRING</u>

(For my little princess)

It's the season of spring
It's a new beginning !
It's the season of spring
It's a new beginning !

With the winter gone,
With the summer coming !
With the winter gone,
With the summer coming !
With the air so clean
With the Sun shining !

It's the season of spring
It's a new beginning !
See the fields all green
See the flowers blooming !
See the fields all green
See the flowers blooming !
Hear the wind-chimes ring,

A Feather In The Breeze

Hear the birdies chirping !

It's the season of spring
It's a new beginning !
Smell the fragrant scents
Smell the fires burning !
Smell the fragrant scents
Smell the fires burning !
Taste the sweetest peas,
Taste the cherries riping !

It's the season of spring
It's a new beginning !
                    Feel this cutest pup
Feel that softest duckling !
                    Feel this cutest pup
Feel that softest duckling !
                All the animals around
Have their new offspring !

It's the season of spring
It's a new beginning !
Oh just look how I jump !
Oh just see how I swing !
Oh just look how I jump !
Oh just see how I swing !

A Feather In The Breeze

This spring-time indeed,

It's a happy feeling !

It's the season of spring
    It's a new beginning !
It's the season of spring
    It's a new beginning !

February 11, 2021

<u>LET MOTHER EARTH HEAL…</u>

Our forefathers got the lion's share
Our fathers got second best
But shall we, the children, ever get…
Mother Earth's blessings choicest ?

Not until we spare a thought
And question the path we tread
Not until we mend our ways
And care for Nature instead…

Trees and forests used to abound
When Earth was in good health
Until we decided to cut them down
To fulfill our greed for wealth !

The oceans and rivers were sparkling clean
And supported all animals and birds
Until we dumped our personal dirt
And damaged them beyond words !

A Feather In The Breeze

The sunshine had that cozy warmth
Back in my grandma's days
But now, it tends to burn me down
With its fiery red sun-rays !

The mountaintops were snow-clad
And beautiful, pristine white !
But I hear that all the glaciers too
Are steadily decreasing in height !

The air doesn't seem clear enough
The raindrops have acidic touch !
Oh, how I miss that clear blue sky
That I used to love so much !

Mother Earth is weeping, badly too
Bearing our misdeeds
And she hopes her children will listen to her,
The ones she lovingly feeds…

Her bounties we have enjoyed a lot
Her nourishment fuels our force
But is it not our duty too…
To replenish our resource ?

A Feather In The Breeze

So let's stop the madness we are in
Let's make the things as before…
Let us start caring for Mother Earth
And restore it's beauty of yore !

April 19, 2021

<u>A FOREST FOR LIFE</u>

A forest indeed is a place "for rest"
For millions of flora and fauna finest
So why should a human ever intrude…
As an ugly, untimely, unwelcome guest ?

A forest protects the soil from erosion
It guards against a flood-like situation
Humans may choose to destroy it all…
But it saves humanity from destruction

It forms the lungs of atmosphere
That help us breathe the freshest of air
But we may lose this useful resource…
Unless we treat it with love and care

Of course, we can't do it in a day
But my words can make a difference, I pray
In helping change a few mindsets...
For letting the existing forests stay

A Feather In The Breeze

And yes, we can choose to sow a seed
Or plant a brand-new sapling indeed
As the path towards a healthy future...
Starts with just one good deed !

June 28, 2021

<u>A TEACHER'S TALE</u>

If I am a tree, you all are my fruits
I am a teacher who strengthens your roots
As a tiny little bud, to me you had come
And look what a lovely flower you've become !

I nourish your brains with good thoughts galore
I correct your mistakes even more
I help you discern the wrongs from the rights
And encourage you to reach new heights !

Although you're the maker of your destiny
You will ever find your well-wisher in me
And mind you when the times are tough
You will always find me close enough !

But as an angel I should not be perceived,
I'm just passing on what I received
As a selfless service to humankind
With all my heart, with all my mind !

A Feather In The Breeze

From you, I ask nothing in return
Life will offer many lessons to learn
Just keep me in your hearts forever
May you succeed in every endeavour !

February 12, 2022